Pray, Slay, & COLLECT.

Beauty is Skin Deep

Presented by:

The Q.U.E.E.N Xperience

Min. Nakita Davis

A Queen Collaboration

JESUS, COFFEE, & PRAYER
Christian Publishing House

MW00976875

Jesus, Coffee, and Prayer Christian Publishing House LLC.

Jesuscoffeeandprayer@gmail.com

400 W. Peachtree St. NW

STE. 4-5055

Atlanta, GA 30308

1.833.333.0733

Editing and typesetting: JESUS, COFFEE, AND PRAYER CHRISTIAN PUBLISHING HOUSE

COVER DESIGN @rebecacovers

Ordering Information: Quantity sales. Special discounts are available on quantity purchases by corporations, associations, and others. For details, contact the publisher: jesuscoffeeandprayer@gmail.com

ISBN 978-1-952273-01-8

DEDICATION

This book is Dedicated to Every WOMAN who has ever been made to feel that she is Only as beautiful as she looks.

Queen~ You are MORE beautiful, MORE talented, MORE resilient, and MORE powerful through Jesus Christ, then You WILL EVER KNOW.

I See YOU Queen & I AM PROUD OF YOU! #KeepShining

~Min Nakita Davis

CEO & Founder

Jesus, Coffee, and Prayer Christian Publishing House LLC.

CONTENTS

PREFACE

Min. Nakita Davis

Smile Queen˜ because you are beautiful.

Laugh Queen˜ because this too shall pass.

Love Queen˜ because you are loved.

The world will try to fill us with filtered fragments, photo chopped portraits, and the imagery of beauty…it's everywhere.

Magazine covers, music videos, movies, our favorite tv-shows, and so much more. As girls, many of us were taught and teach our daughters- **beauty is pain**. Then we wonder why our girls- our young women- and grown women alike continue to stay in toxic- and volatile relationships- at an alarming rate.

Just **maybe**- we subliminally taught them- **pain is beauty & beauty is somehow…love.**

This we know, couldn't be further than the truth.

Truth is ˜ Jesus .is. Love ˜ Jesus .is. Beauty!

The stories, the testimonies, and experiences that my Queens will share with you are designed to give you a fresh perspective and a renewing in Your Spirit.

Prayerfully, we will show you how to **Pray, Slay, & Collect.**

A QUEENS PRAYER

—

Heavenly Father,

We thank you for this divine opportunity to pour into your daughters and the sons who love them. We do not take this opportunity lightly and understand the magnitude of OUR Yes to YOU! Our prayer is that your children will be blessed, transformed, inspired, yet challenged to grow in YOU! Show your daughters the real meaning behind beauty. We count it all joy in advance and Praise you. You are good all by yourself.

Open the spiritual eyes of your readers, open their hearts and minds to receive a word from YOU! We love you Lord and consider it DONE- in the Mighty Name of Jesus Christ we pray.

Amen

Pray, Slay, COLLECT.

Moment of Reflection

How will You Pray Today?

I SEE YOU QUEEN

—

I see you Queen
You stay fly
Hair did- nails did
Everything did
You're the supervisor on the job
You've got your college degree
You pay your own bills and don't need a man for anything

You rock the latest
Your smile is the greatest
Your *Mac* lip gloss matches your purse & your skirt

You're a Boss on so many levels
Many admire you
But what they Can't see
Is what's happening inside of You
You grind in the morning
You grind in the evening
You're building an empire &
That ain't no mistake

But when you're alone
You question who you are
&
What's your life purpose

Your tears are covered by mascara
The internal pain hidden by your rosy blush

You plaster a phony smile & Say
In God we Trust

But I see you Queen
I call you as you Are

Even without the makeup
Beauty Queen-
You are Still a STAR

Just know that Your Sis Is praying for you &
Praying for you to Win
I know you're battling demons- the demons from within

I know you're securing the bag
Putting the coin in the purse
But real beauty is skin deep
That's why I write this verse

~Min. Nakita

Pray, Slay, COLLECT.

Moment of Reflection

How will You Slay Today?

MORE PRECIOUS THAN RUBIES

—

Debora R. Nelson

"She is more precious than rubies; nothing you desire can compare with her. 16 Long life is in her right hand; in her left hand are riches and honor. 17 Her ways are pleasant ways, and all her paths are peace. 18 She is a tree of life to those who take hold of her; those who hold her fast will be blessed."

— Proverbs 3: 15-18

Dear Queen,

You are a true example of a unique, rare, and precious beauty. Your beauty was hand-made, stamped, and packaged *specifically* for you. Who you are and what you bring to the table cannot be duplicated or manifested by anyone other than your *royal* self. Take a moment to remind yourself of the beauty in your skin tone, the beauty in the texture of your hair, and the beauty in your shape. There isn't anyone in this world with your precious image. Your beauty was created by the seeds implanted in you while you were in your mother's womb. You were sprinkled with strength, fierceness, and modesty. Over the years you remained the steward of those seeds and how you water them yields the beautiful masterpiece that others see when they look at you. You are a piece of God's rare and creative art for others to admire. *Your beauty holds value like an antique, it only gets better with time.*

Take a minute to reflect on the moments when you felt the prettiest or when you were one hundred percent content with what you saw when you looked at your reflection in the mirror. I can only imagine that your most beautiful moment was not determined by the fancy shoes that you had on for the evening or that expensive purse that you only pull out on rare occasions. I can only imagine that you saw your truest beauty during the most precious moments of your life. When you were **whole**. Beauty is an outward reflection of the quality of your seeds. How you watered, nurtured, and birth those seeds is represented by the beauty that surrounds you.

Your truest beauty is revealed by the way you care for your mind, body, and soul. Your beauty goal should not be based on the worldly description and vision that is depicted by society. Society equates beauty with materialist factors such as clothing, jewelry, make-up etc. but beauty should be measured by the sharpness of your mind (knowledge and wisdom), your heart (love you display and give), and sprit (your relationship with God). As a former Fashion and Design student at the Philadelphia Art Institute I remember seeking out fashion magazines, art history books, and fashion shows to develop my interpretation of the definition of beauty. I believed that a woman's beauty was based on her size, clothing, and the way she carried herself in high heels. I drew this interpretation based on those things and what I personally perceived as attention grabbers. It wasn't until I experienced life that I realized that an outfit, eye snatching make-up nor high heels made me beautiful.

There were days where I had it all and didn't feel beautiful because I wasn't whole.

It wasn't until I became whole on the inside that I truly believed and felt beautiful and realized that the media had it all wrong! Think about it. There are prominent women in society who we view as one of the most beautiful women on the planet yet they have expressed insecurities and spent thousands of dollars on plastic surgery to fix what they believed to be defects because they did not feel or believe that they were beautiful enough. In some of those cases, plastic surgery caused more of an outward eye sore to others rather than beauty. Once, I came into my wholeness I realized that I had the ability to be beautiful whether I was in a form fitting dress or in sweatpants with a sloppy bun and no make-up! There have been plenty of times where I walked into a room or a store with last minutes clothes thrown on and was told that I was beautiful. But I knew it was only because of the radiance that shined from the inside-out. That shine was a direct reflection of my wholeness. Measuring beauty by your mind, heart, and soul are the true measures of beauty. Even more so, it is equally important to protect and preserve your beauty.

Don't get me wrong, I enjoy putting on the finest clothing and getting dolled up but none of these things define my beauty or make me who I am. Matter of fact ladies, *we make the clothing look good!* WE are the canvas, the foundation of the beauty we bestow!

Develop a lifelong beauty that gradually grows overtime through nurture and care. Gravitating towards like beauty (other people who are whole) and strive to attract, strengthen, and protect your glow! Nurture and protect it so that it may be impossible to ignore!

Beauty Tip

Take care of yourself from the inside out.

Remember: mind, heart, and soul for your internal focus while also implementing a healthy dietary lifestyle. **Start and end** your day with prayer for your soul cleanse. Remember to **love and show love** daily- it minimizes wrinkles and keeps a smile on your face as well as others. Take some time to read to keep your mind sharp, join a book club or create your own book list. Finally, the outward appearance- exercise, exercise, exercise. Make time for a great workout. Not only will it keep your outer appearance intact, it's also a great stress reliever!

Beauty Secret

My must have "Beauty-Secret" .... WATER!

I drink plenty of water to keep my skin clear. Our skin is the outer shell of our beauty. Believe it or not, allowing your skin to breathe can sometimes have a more lasting effect.

Oh, and *eyebrows!*

You can take on the world with *fierce brows*. I absolutely love the ˜Anastasia Brow Wiz˜ It's great for filling and shaping your eyebrows with a natural touch!

SLAY in business

I make it a priority to wake-up early enough to work-out, of course shower, and take precious time to do my hair, light make-up, and make sure my uniform is crisp and ready to take on the world as an active duty officer in the US Army. As a woman in the Army I find it to be extremely important for women to maintain their femininity in a male dominated profession.

My beauty mantra at work:

"Be an asset to any project your assigned while looking good doing it!" #howiSlay

I make it a priority to ensure that I am in tip top shape, skin is glowing, and **hair is maintained like a crown** (meaning with care and attention to detail.)

Collect

I collect by starting and ending each day with prayer.

I've recently made it a habit to wake up an hour earlier to allow time for listening to an empowering worship song to get my mind in the right place. During my travels to and from work, nine times out of ten I am listening to either a Sarah Jakes message or a self-help book on Audible. I've been primarily focused on *feeding my mind positive vibes and energy.*

I am nothing and can do nothing without God.

I know this, therefore the primary source that keeps me grounded is my faith and relationship with God. I also make time to chat with family, close friends, and my significant other. They give me balance and I love it. I am such a goal driven person, so when I'm not at work I'm usually at home knocking out personal goals. That keeps me going! Lastly, I protect my peace by being *selective* when it comes to the company that I keep. I preserve my energy by sticking to my planner and encourage myself by reading material that causes me to stretch outside of my comfort zone.

Three additional gems for the ladies

1. Know and walk in your value and worth: you were put on this earth for a reason. There is an assignment with your name on it and who you are and what you bring to the table is enough to get it done! Have **confidence**.

2. Never allow a relationship or marriage to define your beauty: Before you entered the relationship or marriage you were beautiful, you are beautiful now, and **you will always be beautiful.**

3. Look yourself in the mirror daily and remind yourself of you who you are, where you've come from, and where you're going: **You are a Queen, carry yourself like it my Royal friend.**

About the Author

Published 2x Bestselling Author Debora R. Nelson, MBA is a native of Egg Harbor Township, New Jersey and currently serves as an active duty Captain in the United States Army. When not serving her country, she can be found building her clothing empire as the CEO & Designer of Debora's Custom Clothier or ripping the runway. Debora is an aspiring motivational speaker who is dedicated to igniting purpose in the lives of others. If you're interested in Debora's keys to success ~purchase: ***30-week guide to creating Unconditional Success*** on Amazon or Barnes and Noble.com

<u>Stay Connected with this Pray, Slay, & Collect Queen</u>

Email <u>Debora.r.nelson@gmail.com</u> TN: 254.432.2307

Follow on Facebook: Debora R. Nelson or Author's Page @Ms. Debora R. Nelson

Instagram: @discussion_with_deb

"SECURE THE BAG QUEEN- BUT NEVER FORGET WHO MADE THE BAG! #GOD" ~ MIN. NAKITA

Pray, Slay, COLLECT.
Moment of Reflection

How will You Collect Today?

Prepare a Table

—

Tenesa Mobley

"You prepare a table before me in the presence of my enemies. You anoint my head with oil; my cup overflows. Surely your goodness and love will follow me all the days of my life, and I will dwell in the house of the Lord forever."

— Psalms 23:5-6

The most valuable thing I've done in my life was fall in love with me. Growing up as a middle child and only girl I felt the need to always fight for my place or make myself feel relevant. So, at an early age I took on the responsibility of being the protector and caregiver to my brothers. That made me feel wanted and needed. I valued my worth on how well I cooked for them and being there as a nurture. Little did I know, I was setting myself up to value the opinions my family and friends more than I did me. During my teenage years I wanted to be the person that everyone else that I should be instead of figuring out who I really wanted to be.

Entering college, I took that mindset with me. When I got pregnant in the summer of my upcoming sophomore year, I began to develop the attitude that it wasn't about others, but it was about me. My mindset began to *change*. It was during that time, that I realized that I will never please everyone~ no matter how much right I did for them.

I had to start living my life.

I had another life that I was now responsible for and I wanted to live a life where my child could see me with *love pride and joy*. I wanted my child to see me and **not** everyone else when they looked into my eyes. It was time for me to live my life in a way which was befitting to me and my happiness.

It was time for me to find me.

Upon discovering who I am, I realized some things that I've been taught as child or told to do as a child had no place in my life. Many black cultures are taught that when something isn't right within the family you should just *"sweep it under the rug."*

I had to learned that "sweeping it under the rug" is **not a solution**. That's a cowardly way out.

There's no resolution with that theory. Nothing ever gets fixed and if it's not properly discussed then it leads to greater issues in the future. No one should silence their voice just to go along to get along. I learned that my voice as a child was just as important as an adult. It was then that I realized that no matter how happy I tried to make others that **even in my childhood I owned my voice** ~ no matter how many times people tried to take it away. I wanted my child to know that he has a voice as well~ stand firm on your principles. As a result of getting pregnant out of wedlock, many tried to force marriage down my throat.

If I had the same mindset that I had as a teenager, I would have done so. But because I was beginning to truly love and adore me, I had to do what made me happy. Marrying my child's father was not an option. Although I loved him, I was *starting to love myself more.*

Mentally and emotionally, I knew that I deserved. At that time, he was incapable of doing that; we were incapable of providing an environment conducive to a child.

Collect

I chose to be a single mother and use the strength God gave me to make sure all my child's needs were met. I knew my child would benefit more from being raised in a home with one parent, full of love, positivity, and happiness, opposed to being in a toxic two-parent household.

Yes, I was frowned upon for being a young single mother.

Every stone thrown at me, I *collected* each of them and built a marble fortress. It made me tougher, stronger and more determined to show people my capabilities as a mother and a woman.

Those stones *prepared* me for the upset and let downs of life.

It was my determination and my faith in God that got me through abusive relationships.

The hurt of being told by someone who said he love me that I wasn't good enough ~ smart enough ~ pretty enough; the hurt of being told that people only associated with me because of my light skin; the hurt of being told that I will NEVER amount to anything; all of these things only made me LOVE Me More.

I continued to lift my head up and smile.

I realized that I loved me so much, that I refused to allow someone who didn't even love themselves, to dictate who I Am or my Destiny.

God created me to be the best me.

My Father said "thou preparest a table before me in the presence of mine enemies. Surely goodness and mercy shall follow me all the days of my life."

Because I know who my Father is, and I believe what my Father says ~words from man CAN'T Destroy My Confidence.

The more people tried to destroy me the more God elevated and blessed me!

I had to learn

The more I found me, the more people I lost along the way. In those moments, I discovered the real meaning of friendship, loyalty, and trust. I discovered that people don't value you. They only value what you can provide for them at that time.

I was once told years ago "Fake friends are like fall leaves, you can find them anywhere. Real friends are like diamonds precious and rare." The older I got; I began to really understand that meaning. I began to really appreciate and value my true friends. Some people I've outgrown and I'm okay with that.

I realized that this journey that my Father is taking me on, everyone is not designed to go with me. Some people have a hard time letting go of people in their circle because of history or a sense of obligation.

I had to learn that some history and obligations are only dead weight.

Dead weight will only hold you back, bring you down, and keep you from your GREATNESS!

I made the decision to choose me because I AM worth all the Greatness that my Father has in store for me.

This is my beauty story!

About the author

Tenesa Mobley is the only girl of 3 brothers; raised in Eutaw (Greene County) Alabama. She is the proud mother of one child Jay. He is her world, motivation, and strength. She currently resides in Gwinnett County, Georgia.

Stay Connected with this Pray, Slay, & Collect Queen

IG @Msmobley1

Prayer

Forgive us Lord, for putting anything before you. If it's the vanity of our looks, our career, business, tangible items or self. Help us to see the error in our ways. Help us to keep the focus on you. Do this with your generous grace and abounding love.

Amen

Min.Nakita

Pray, Slay, COLLECT.

Moment of Reflection

What will You Pray for Today?

FEARFULLY AND WONDERFULLY MADE

Dr. Tonya Blackmon

"I praise you because I am fearfully and wonderfully made; your works are wonderful, I know that full well."

— Psalm 139:14 (NIV)

As a youngster, I was surrounded by beautiful women. I watched my Aunts wear long gowns, detailed wigs and perfect makeup in their photo shoots. I remember watching my Mom apply Fashion Fair makeup and bright red lipstick before she would dress to go out with my Dad or her sisters. To this day, she takes a warm, wet cloth and laces it with Vaseline before she applies it to her face. To my knowledge, she has only used ivory to clean her face. I have never seen a pimple on my Mom's face. Back then, I thought beauty meant looking your best and wearing your best.

Then, I grew up and disagreed with the old cliché that states beauty is only skin deep.

Being beautiful is more than physical attributes.

The perfect eye color, body shape, hair length, etc. does not exist. Society and trends will try to sell us lies and dictate how the ideal, beautiful woman should look. However, the scriptures do a superb job of explaining the true *essence of beauty*.

Psalm 139:14 (NIV) states "I praise you because I am fearfully and wonderfully made; your works are wonderful, I know that full well."

Our maker knew exactly what he was doing when he made his creation. We can find joy in knowing that his creation (US) was magnificently modeled.

We are beautiful.

I first realized my beauty when I was young. I remember hearing my Mom brag about her three beautiful girls. Yet, as I became a teenager, I would compare myself with other young, more popular girls. A seed of low self-esteem developed, and it was not until I started **reading and applying** the word of God to my life that I found comfort in Psalm 139:14.

I began to read more scriptures about how much God loves me and learned that physical beauty fades over time, but good character and a loving spirit are everlasting.

Today, when I look in the mirror, I love every part of my body.

One of my eyes is larger than the other, *but I thank God that I have great sight.*

My natural hair is kinky and a little grey, *but I thank God that I have hair.*

I am 4 feet 10 inches tall, *but I thank God that I can stretch my arms to 5 feet 11 inches.*

I cannot sing like Yolanda Adams, *but my prayers are powerful, and they do reach the heaven lines.*

I wake up each day and see a beautiful woman in the mirror.

Beauty tip

Natural Scrub to exfoliate lips: Mix ½ teaspoon sugar and 5-8 drops of Vitamin E oil. Gently rub on lips. Wipe off scrub and apply lip balm.

As a business professional, I have the awesome job of inspiring women to transform their lives and the businesses they have always dreamed about!

About the author

Dr. Tonya B. is a Veteran, consultant, podcast host, grant writer, and sought-after speaker. She inspires and educates Big businesses to achieve their dreams by developing strategic plans, in-depth research, and leveraging her wealth of knowledge. She holds her PHD. in International Business studies.

Stay Connected with this Pray, Slay, & Collect Queen

Business Name: Conglomerate Empowerment

FB Handle: https://www.facebook.com/tonyasblessed

IG Handle: https://www.instagram.com/drtonyablive/

Website: https://congempowerment.biz/

Prayer

God- we trust you. You are the Author and Perfecter of our faith. Help us to be bold like Esther and glean like Ruth. Help us to follow your instructions like Mary.

Let us not be in haste like Martha. Order our steps even now and we will be so humbled to give you all the Praise and Glory forever!

Amen

Min. Nakita

Pray, Slay, COLLECT.

Moment of Reflection

What challenge will You Slay Today?

UNFADING BEAUTY

—

Angela Foxworth

"Your beauty should not come from outward adornment, such as elaborate hairstyles and the wearing of gold jewelry or fine clothes. Rather, it should be that of your inner self, the unfading beauty of a gentle and quiet spirit, which is of great worth in God's sight."

— 1 Peter 3:3-4

People say beauty is only skin deep. 1 Peter 3:3-4 says it all!

Beauty is not your high fashion image of the best hair products; the perfectly worn makeup or body enhancements. *True beauty is what lies within you.*

In short; your heart.

How you treat people is a true indicator of beauty. Living your life to help others and being a positive example to everyone you come across is a beautiful way to be. You can be the most aesthetically beautiful woman in the world, but not if you treat people poorly and are self-absorbed.

Somehow, these qualities do not allow your beauty to shine through. We all have different characteristics/traits that we feel make us beautiful. In my experience, **confidence** has been the most attractive feature a woman can wear.

It *overrides* how pretty your face is, how long your legs are or how aesthetically put together you are. Looks are just a surface satisfaction.

Your character is everlasting.

The importance of being a dynamic leader in whatever it is you set out to accomplish supersedes how well you look playing the part. Remember, *beauty fades with age.* There must be substance lying underneath; especially, after the initial eye contact has been satisfied.

Questions to ask yourself?

- Are you able to have a real dialogue about many subjects in life?
- Do you like to let your hair down and show your more natural side sometimes?
- Do you give of your time to someone less fortunate?

These are actions of substance.

This is how we SLAY!!!

My definition of SLAY is a Sassy Lady Always Yielding.

It means that I am productive, confident and fun!

I am looked at as a Queen and a trendsetter; someone to look up to. I am always on the grind, and my strength in God is my Super-POWER.

There is no one like me! (or You Either!)

I am unique and I was created to do EXACTLY what I am doing. *This mindset is how you win in life.*

We must truly believe in what we are doing, who we are, and what we want to accomplish. This mindset is also what makes you a BOSS! *A Bold and Optimistic Sexy Sensation!*

When you operate in the calling that has been placed on your life, everything else just falls into place.

The expression is called "staying in your lane." Each and every one of us has been created for our own unique purpose. Only you know what that is. When you operate in your designed purpose, positive things happen.

Your beauty is how you handle the challenges in life, how you endure through the tough times and celebrate the victories!

You will have many of those.

We love the rewards of hard work.

I truly believe that when you *find* the thing that you are most passionate about, your success becomes inevitable.

Collect

Doing what you love will allow you to make money. Your purpose really makes room for your financial status in life. When you **focus on your purpose** the *paycheck will follow*. Most women get sidetracked when they don't know who they are. How are you able to succeed if you don't know what it is you need to be doing? Refuse to settle for what is convenient and do the 'thing' that you are passionate about!

Dropping your fear is a huge part of moving forward in your success.

#FACTS

I am *scared* most of the time when I am pursuing something that is outside of the box and that no one else understands.

No one ever said that you would not get scared…you must continue *moving forward* even in your fear. The more you accomplish in doing that, the stronger you will be.

Strength and faith are attractive qualities and attributes that add to your overall beauty. *There is nothing more attractive than a woman who does not let failures defeat her.* This makes her extremely powerful. In addition, consistent evolution and timing are extremely important factors as you continue your journey.

Ultimately, the formula will match, and the bank account will hatch!

The importance of being an effective leader in your business is so much bigger than just you. People are watching you. There are young girls that are watching your every move and look up to you.

There are women your age who need to see the success of what you are doing so that they can follow your footsteps.

We are equipped to leave a legacy for our family and their families. True success is not measured in the length of your hair, the color of your skin, or even the size of your body. Those attributes are superficial and temporary to say the least. Knowing your worth, being confident in your business, and being an example to women all around you are long lasting attributes that will carry on long after you have passed away.

I write this to encourage and inspire Every single woman out there! Never let your age, looks or financial status detour you from living out your dreams~ they will come true.

There have been many times that I have personally wanted to throw in the towel, but I had to remember the word of God. Ecclesiastes 9:11 says, "The race is not given to the swift nor the strong but he who endures until the end."

Sis, It does not matter how early or late you get started, JUST Move and believe that You Can Do It!

Life with A. Fox is living outside the box and my success has been rooted in my Faith in God and knowing what He has purposed me to do.

That is a beauty that lasts forever.

About the author

Angela Foxworth is an International talk show host, journalists, and media personality positioned to make a positive difference. She is the reigning Mrs. Georgia Woman US Majesty 2020 and loves to travel, sing and dance. She believes coming together and finding common ground is the only way to prosper. She currently resides in Marietta, Georgia with her husband, 2 children and her first born grandson.

Stay Connected with this Pray, Slay, & Collect Queen

Visit: www.theafoxhow.com

FB@ The Real A Fox

Pray, Slay, COLLECT.

Moment of Reflection

What will You Collect Today?

OVERCOME BY THE BLOOD OF THE LAMB

Leela Diaz

"And they overcame him by the blood of the Lamb, and by the word of their testimony: and they loved not their lives unto the death."

— Revelation 12:11 KJV

Understanding that we have, "Overcome by the blood of the Lamb and the word of our testimony...."

When the Lord first spoke to me on starting this business, I heard from Him that not only would these products work for me, but that I would use my testimony.

Your testimony is incredibly powerful, considering it to be the means by which you may overcome. I do, however, love the fact that «overcome » or « conquered » (as many versions read) is written in past tense. Jesus has already won the victory on the cross through his death and resurrection so that we may conquer or « slay » in all that we are called to do!

The Bible says in 1 Samuel 16 that "Man looks at the outward appearance, but the Lord looks on the heart."

Clearly, what is in your heart is what matters the most. However, man does judge outward appearance, which is why first impressions are important. I don't know about you, but I would like favor with God AND man! Just as Esther from the Bible prepared herself with beauty treatments, her appearance opened the door for the King to marry her.

I realized my own beauty when I began to see myself as the Bible defines me, which is "fearfully and wonderfully made."

Growing up, I did not feel good about myself.

I was overweight, had acne, braces, and glasses. *I think you get the picture!* Of course, establishing a relationship with Christ changed the way I valued myself.

Through the years, I learned how to put myself together. God loves us and wants us to take care of ourselves because we have *worth*.

I was inspired by the 'Spirit of excellence' that Daniel had as the Bible describes in Daniel 6:3 ESV. Meditating on this helps me keep my composure. It also ties correlates closely with my business and as it pertains to beauty and appearance.

I market natural products designed to assist with weight loss, sugar and carb cravings, boosting energy, and releasing all 4 'Happy Hormones' including Dopamine, Oxytocin, Seratonin, and Endorphines. The staple of these products is called **Happy Coffee** also known as *Skinny Coffee* or *Smart Coffee*.

When your body is in proper alignment from these happy hormones being released, it can actually self-correct imbalances ~ Hence the name *Smart Coffee*. The other products (which accomplish the same goal) are a cocoa, a lemonade, and another specialized coffee.

Being in this state of mind (where my happy hormones are being released), positions me for worship. I have even heard other believers report similar experiences!

I hope to inspire other women who have struggled with their weight and self-confidence. I truly desire to see others be the best version of themselves! There are many people who, despite proper diet and exercise, fail to lose weight. Or perhaps they might live with chronic pain, a thyroid issue or another health condition. While i can never prescribe, there are countless testimonies from people who have been greatly helped by this same product! As for myself, it has completely transformed my metabolism, and given me a new energy and focus.

For many years I had a thyroid problem, felt sluggish, and struggled with my weight. *Happy Coffee* has greatly assisted me in my weight loss, reduced bloating, and allowed me to eat more of what I want without gaining excess weight! The desire of my heart is to do the same for others.

3 John 2:1 NKJV reads,

"Beloved, I pray that you may prosper in all things, and be in good health, just as your soul prospers."

Nothing says it better than the Word of God.

His desire is for us to prosper in every way! It is so incredibly rewarding to hear back from customers on how their health has improved. Whether they lost 50 pounds, or joint pain is gone, or even feel closer to the Lord, I am thankful to be a part of their story.

It is a joy to use my gift to bless other people.

Beauty Secret

If you're like me, you are pleased with your look at 9:00am~ your make-up is still fresh. However, by mid-afternoon, you may struggle with your face shining too bright (and not in a spiritual way!)

Inexpensive and natural quick fix:

By throwing rolled oats into a food processor for approximately 2 minutes, you will have a light flour that can be used as a loose facial powder. (Yes!!!, oat flour can be used in cooking too, but either way it's fast and hassle free.)

#howiSlay

I start out my day with my *Happy Coffee*, which gets me moving and feeling ready to #slay! I have borrowed lots of organization advice and Biblical principles from *Terri Savelle Foy*. Surrounding yourself with wise counselors, as the Bible advises, also includes godly mentors who know how to slay in Business or Ministry.

One of King David's secrets was praising God and remaining in joy.

I've found that my level of joy greatly impacts how efficient I am in my work. Psalm 16:11 ESV says, "...in your presence is fullness of joy; at your right hand are pleasures forevermore." Nehemiah 8:10 NIV mentions, "... the joy of the Lord is your strength. "

In the same way that David slew Goliath, if we stay in joy, the Lord will strengthen and anoint us to slay our own giants too!

About the Author

Leela Diaz is a Woman of God with a savvy business spirit. She holds a Master's degree and enjoys proclaiming the Good News of Jesus Christ. She is a loving wife and mother.

Stay Connected with this Pray, Slay, & Collect Queen

Business Name: Happy Coffee

FB Handle: https://www.facebook.com/leela.jadhav.7

IG Handle: https://www.instagram.com/leela.diaz/

Website: leeladiaz.com

Pray, Slay, COLLECT.

Moment of Reflection

Who will You Pray for Today?

God's Masterpiece

—

Sheena Floyd

"For we are God's masterpiece. He has created us anew in Christ Jesus, so we can do the good things he planned for us long ago."

Ephesians 2:10 NLT

Knowing your worth, your purpose, and living by your own standards vs society's measures is *true beauty*.

Pretty comes a dime a dozen but what's rare and inimitable is a pretty soul.

"We delight in the beauty of the butterfly, but rarely admit the changes it has gone through to achieve that beauty" Maya Angelou.

It took lots of prayer and faking it before I could look in the mirror and truly say "Wow Sheena you have it going on!" Like most people, I dealt with the stress of not feeling smart enough, pretty enough, or even successful enough when comparing myself to others. *I had a timeline on my life and when it wasn't met, I felt the pressure.* And with that pressure, came bad decisions and a mean version of myself.

If I could talk to my teenage self I would say:

Repeat after me, "You are a masterpiece (Ephesians 2:10) You are fearfully and wonderfully made (Psalms 139.14)" Now say it every day until you believe it. One day you will look in the mirror and **LOVE** the person you see. Not because of what you look like but because of how hard you have worked to be the person you are on the inside. There will be women prettier than you, more successful than you but let me tell you this, your giving spirit, your hard work, and your love for the Lord is what will define you and your beauty!

No one can take that away.

As you navigate this life, know **"it's already done."** Your path has already been created and you have a special relationship with the Lord. You don't know it yet, but Jesus Christ will be the one that helps you through some of the most difficult times in your life. Its Jesus that's going to **keep you** up during those long stressful nights as you finish that Master's degree.

Its Jesus that's going to **promote** you to a new position just when you start to feel defeated in your current position.

Stay humble, ignore the nay-sayers, and walk with purpose.

Just when you feel like your life is off track, and YOUR plan isn't working, Jesus will show you His plan. Start digging those ditches (2kings 3:16) because the desires of your heart will be received. Don't let anyone tell you differently. Take care of your skin, spend the extra dollars on a good moisturizer, drink lots of water and watch your life flourish! Delayed does not mean denied! Trust in God, trust His process. And in the words of my forever First Lady, when life gets hard, "stay true to yourself and never let what somebody says distract you from your goals." ~Michelle Obama

Beauty Tip

Stress causes wrinkles, so I live by this...

"If it doesn't make you happy DON'T Do It!"

-

Beauty Must haves

Urban skin Rx, Sweet Comb Chicago lip balm, and Mac Ruby woo lipstick.

#howiSlay

A **bold** lip, a **fierce** outfit, and an **open** heart is how I slay!

Prayer

Father God,

I pray that everyone reading this is blessed with the confidence you have instilled in them. I pray that all women, truly know their self-worth and have the confidence to navigate this life knowing that they are fearfully and wonderfully made, and you did NOT make any mistakes. I pray that whatever standards the world tries to put on our young girls, when they look in the mirror, they see what you see, a *Masterpiece*.

In Jesus Name, I pray
Amen!!!

About the author

Sheena Floyd has an impressive career in corporate leadership and training for a Fortune Top 10 organization. Her MBA studies and unique ability to connect with adult learners has afforded her opportunities to travel the world.

Stay Connected with this Pray, Slay, & Collect Queen

FB @sheenafloyd

Pray, Slay, COLLECT.

Moment of Reflection

How will You Slay in Your home and business/career Today?

ACCORDING TO HIS PURPOSE

—

Sheraton Gatlin

"And we know that all things work together for good to them that love God, to them who are the called according to his purpose."

— Romans 8:28 (KJV)

When I first moved to Atlanta in 2012, I wasn't happy with myself at all. I thought I was, until I got around what seemed to be the typical "woman from Atlanta." It seemed that the women from Atlanta had a *specific* look. The men also thought so. I had no idea what I was getting myself into.

I loved Atlanta for the opportunities and diversity. Everybody was focused on being successful in some shape, form, or fashion. I had never been around so many driven individuals. I started exploring the city, trying new things, and attending events to meet new people. I remember a gentleman walking up to me and asking me where I was from. He proceeded to say that he knew I wasn't from Atlanta. I asked him "why is that?" He responded that women from Atlanta had a specific look and I did not fit the profile. At this time, I couldn't figure out if this was compliment or an insult.

Now I can't lie, during this time, my weight was heavily on my mind. My cousin and her friends that I hung out with were all a slimmer build. Everyone was working out.

I felt like the friend that was overweight.

Basically, "the fat" girl of the crew.

I wasn't happy about being so called "thick" anymore.

I started working out daily. I changed my entire diet. Eating mainly fish and salad. I would snack on yogurt, baked chips, and 100 calorie cookies. Drinking much more water. I lost a total of 30 pounds and became more content~ more comfortable in my clothes.

But what happens when you're still *broken?*

Hurting on the inside while the outside is shining?

The Bible says:

"Your beauty should not come from outward adornment, such as elaborate hairstyles and the wearing of gold jewelry or fine clothes. Rather, it should be that of your inner self, the unfading beauty of a gentle and quiet spirit, which is of great worth in God's sight."

1 Peter 3:3-4 NIV

It's not about how well you can dress it up, but rather, genuine happiness and true confidence.

Real authentic beauty is intangible and exudes from within.

I finished at *Gwynnis Mosby Makeup academy* in 2015. I had to find my way in a new world of creatives. My family and friends use to ask me to do their hair and makeup, but I never saw it as my craft.

Shortly after finishing the academy, I had to come up with a brand and a name to go by. A name that I could envision *globally*. After brainstorming and tossing around ideas with my old supervisor, I came up with *VoirBelle, LLC.*

It's French for *"to see or to behold beautiful."*

My desire is to *enhance* that beauty of every individual that I touch as a contributor in the makeup industry. I am fulfilled when my clients gaze into the mirror and "see beautiful." Sometimes, I get a smile and at other times, tears of joy.

In my line of work, I can meet individuals who simply need their beauty to be *dusted off* a bit. Their beauty has always been there, but maybe they have not *seen* or felt it in a while.

It's my job to dust it off and bring that beauty back to life.

#howiSlay

My *true beauty* is realized, every single day that I conquer, whatever life throws my way.

My true beauty is realized, when I begin to see my dreams come true.

My true beauty is realized, when I see my *growth, progress,* and my blessed ability to excel when others spit in my face!

My *character* is beauty.

My *spirit* is beauty,

My *heart* and *soul* are beauty.

I now realize that whether big or small ~*God is within me.*

That is my true beauty!

So God created mankind in his own image, in the image of God he created them; male and female he created them.

Genesis 1:27 | NIV

The gentleman that asked me if I was from Atlanta ended up telling me that all the women in Atlanta looked the same, dress the same, as well as wear their hair the same. I stood out to him because I didn't look like everybody else.

Sis realize that your *uniqueness* and *confidence* is beauty.

Favour is deceitful, and beauty is vain:

but a woman that feareth the Lord, she shall be praised.

Proverbs 31:30 | KJV

Beauty tip

What's within will glow through your skin!

Be sure to take good care of your skin.

Wash your face daily.

Exfoliate a minimum of 3 times per week; if you add another day it's ok, but don't overdo it.

Be sure to moisturize your skin.

And PLEASE don't forget to clean your makeup brushes!

YES, clean them! When you do this **and** drink plenty water, **Queen you are ready to rock!**

Beauty Secret revealed by VoirBelle

If I had to be completely honest, one of my best kept Beauty Secrets is **Vaseline**! #MustHave

This is a product I use *faithfully* every day.

Most people ask if it clogs up my pores, but I honestly can say that I do not experience this issue. It's been a product I've using since I was a kid. I'd like to thank my mother and father, Mr. & Mrs. Warren Reed for that! -insert smile-

Truthfully, it works for me great; especially when seasons change. I am able to avoid dry patches on my face. Only a light coat of it goes on my face.

I'd take it over a body lotion any day!

#howiSlay

"You may encounter many defeats, *but you must not be de-feated*. *In fact, it **may be necessary to encounter the de-***

feats, *so* **you** can know who **you** are, what **you** can rise from, how **you** can still come out of it." - *Maya Angelou*

I **choose** not to be defeated and I **choose** not to look like what I'm going through. I understand and accept that I am human; I make mistakes, I live, and I will learn.

But I only have one life to live.

I **choose** to break generational curses and live out my purpose.

Therefore, I make time for my DREAM.

I plan to give my parents and my son all their flowers while here on earth, in addition to blessing many other individuals.

Pursuing my *dreams*, sometimes means sleepless and restless nights, met by the early mornings. A lot of times it's *compromise* and *sacrifice*. I have shed blood, sweat, and tears.

No matter what, I continue to believe in me.

I've been blessed beyond measure by the relationships I've built, the encounters, the people I've met, and the experiences that I will never forget while pursuing my passion within the beauty industry.

My gift has made room for me and it has also taken me internationally as a makeup artist to places I thought I'd never go. I look forward to all the things that God is doing within my life as I continue to grow both personally and professionally in my beauty business!

About the author

Sheraton Gatlin is a published makeup artist and a rising star in the makeup and beauty industry. She has achieved countless accomplishments and has worked with noted filmmakers such as **Jasmine Burke**, celebrity actors such as **Richard Tyson** of *"Kindergarten Cop"* and **Tray Chaney**, *Kendrick* of Bounce TVs "Saint and Sinners" and *Poot* of "The Wire" just to name a few. As an International & Celebrity Makeup artist, Sheraton is quickly becoming a household name that you won't soon forget!

Stay Connected with this Pray, Slay, & Collect Queen

VoirBelle, LLC.

FB Handle: VoirBelle by Sheraton

IG Handle: @voirbelle

Website: www.voirbelle.com

Prayer

Heavenly Father,

Let your daughters know that they are LOVED! No filter, No mascara, No lipstick required.

They are not their job. Their businesses, or just a wife or mother. Let them know that they have an Even Higher calling over their lives.

You call them a child of God! Plant seeds of spiritual growth- mind, body, and soul even now.

In Jesus Name we Pray

Amen

Min. Nakita

Pray, Slay, COLLECT.

Moment of Reflection

How will You Collect Your Joy Today?

REVERENCE GOD

Rev. Tiffany Bellamy-Lyles

"Charm can be deceptive and beauty doesn't last, but a woman who fears and reverences God shall be greatly praised."

— Proverbs 31:30 TLB

I haven't always been the most confident and quite honestly, if I was still relying on my outer appearance, some days I would still waiver.

I can remember growing up and admiring other females for their beauty. *Truthfully, I never felt beautiful enough.* Many times, I felt like the caterpillar that would never blossom into a beautiful butterfly. By the time I turned 27, I had *recreated* myself by conforming to what the world considered to be beautiful. I would get my hair done and purchase the nicest, tightest dress with heels, just to dance in the mirror and get drunk at the club.

I was so vain that I literally danced looking in the mirror all night. It did my heart good to know I was a head turner. I even turned my nose up on other women who I felt didn't look as good. However, when I was by myself something was missing.

In all honesty, I was so ugly and vile on the inside.

I continued this lifestyle for about a year or so, until one day I was introduced to someone very *special*. It was someone who loved me for who I really was. It was someone who introduced me to *true beauty*.

It was my Father, my God.

Pray

As I began to indulge in Him spending time in the *Word and* **prayer**, God started to speak to me. He told me that the clothes, shoes, hair, and shape didn't define me, but what's inside of me does.

No matter how beautiful I was on the outside I was very unattractive on the inside.

I'm so grateful that the God I serve looks at the heart of all and not the outside. God knew what I longed for and what I needed, and He gave that to me. He gave me affirmation and confirmation of who I really was. In that instance beauty meant something totally different to me.

Some months ago I spoke to a lady and she spoke back. She continued to stare at me and say, "You are so beautiful" repeatedly. All I could do was smile. That night God reminded me that the beauty she saw was coming from the inside out ~ my newly found *true* beauty.

God transformed me! His glory was shining so radiantly that it placed the lady in awe! Little did she know she was in *awe* of God.

I discovered that I gained my true essence of beauty by accepting the Lord Jesus Christ as my personal Lord and Savior and entering a *personal relationship* with Him. I learned to stand **firm, trust, and believe** every word He spoke to me about me.

He told me I was fearfully and wonderfully MADE, which meant I was already beautiful when He created me.

Beauty Secret Tip revealed

I cleanse myself daily in the Lord. Emptying myself of *Tiffany* and allowing God to fill me up with more of Him.

Beauty #MustHave

Lip gloss has always been a must have for me because people can see your smile from a far. The shiner the lips the more noticeable the smile. #shine

#howiSlay

Each morning I pray and ask God to direct my paths.

With a *smile* on my face, my short cut, a *bubbly personality*, and shining *lip gloss*, I go out into the world. I work full time, go to school events, church, and spend time with my family.

God makes a way to balance it all because I center my day around Him.

My mission is to bring light to at least one person each day, as *I hope I brought light to you!*

Prayer

Father God we love and honor You.

Right now, Lord God, I speak life into the Woman of God that is reading this at this very moment. Father God help her to see her the way that **You** *see her. The world looks at beauty entirely different from the way You do, so I declare and decree in the sweet name of Jesus our sacrificial lamb, that this* **beautiful Woman of God receives a crown of beauty for her ashes***. But most importantly accepts the Lord Jesus Christ as her personal Lord and Savior.*

Amen

About the author

Reverend Tiffany Bellamy-Lyles is a loving wife, mother of 5 amazing children, business career woman and most importantly~ the Beautiful daughter of a King! She is passionate about spreading the Good News of Jesus Christ and looks forward to all God has instore for His sons and daughters in this season!

<u>Stay Connected with this Pray, Slay, & Collect Queen</u>

Follow on FB @ Tiffany Bellamy-Lyles

"Keep your heels high & your FAITH higher"
~ Min. Nakita

Pray, Slay, COLLECT.

Moment of Reflection

How will You Show Your Inside Beauty Today?

BE BLESSED

LoWanda "Dee" Davis

"Wherever you go and whatever you do, you will be blessed."

— Deuteronomy 28:6 NLT

Beauty to me is not all about the appearance of a person but their true inner qualities.

I realized my *real* beauty after I accepted Christ in my life. Before that time, I thought beauty was just about how I looked; however, having Christ helped me to realize that my real beauty was on the inside.

Growing up, I remember my grandmother telling me, "It doesn't matter how pretty you are, if you have a bad attitude it still makes you ugly."

That one statement helped me as well to understand that inner beauty is most important. With all that I've learned it's so valuable to know that it's more important to work on your inner beauty than your outer beauty.

Beauty Tip

Never let your outward beauty outweigh your inward beauty

Beauty Secret #MustHave

Sei Bella Lip gloss

#howiSlay

Work the LOOK don't let the LOOK work you!

Prayer

Lord keep me humble from day to day.

Please allow my inward beauty to grow so that it may be equal to or greater than my outward beauty.

Amen

About the author

Lowanda "Dee" Davis is a Woman of God, Veteran, Playwright, and serial entrepreneur. She is a blessing to many that she encounters!

Stay Connected with this Pray, Slay, & Collect Queen

Follow on FB @ Lowanda Dee Davis

"A FRESH SHOWER, A PRAYER, & SOME LIP GLOSS GOES A LONG WAY." ~ MIN. NAKITA

Pray, Slay, COLLECT.

Moment of Reflection

How will You help another Queen Slay (get it done) Today?

God's Handiwork

—

Tamika Morrow

"For we are God's Handiwork created in Christ Jesus to do good work, which God has prepared in advance for us to do."

— Esphesians 2:10

Beauty to me is the simple act of just being yourself. Loving and accepting yourself just as you are *makes* you beautiful. True beauty comes from having *confidence* in yourself~ feeling comfortable in your *own skin* while appreciating your flaws.

Psalms 13:9-14 says, "I praise you because I am fearfully and wonderfully made: your works are wonderful, I know that full well." So that tells me that we are created in the image of God and we all know that **God don't make no junk!** #nojunk

Beauty is a mindset. We must remind ourselves daily.

Looking back, I see now that I didn't realize my own TRUE beauty until I started the journey of becoming a Best version and moving more *effective* in my ministry. I had to rid my mind of negative thoughts that had mentally attached themselves to me for years.

Hearing people in my circle and family say negative things about my looks in my younger years inadvertently hurt my self-esteem. It turned me into a woman that felt was not beautiful enough at times.

I can still remember the pain felt behind a family members cruel statement to me. That family member had just completed a photoshoot and now we were both looking at the final pictures. I remember seeing one of the photos and complementing my family on how very beautiful and bold they looked in one picture.

Instead of graciously saying 'Thank you.' That family member screamed "Ewwww! I look like you in this picture!"

This was not only spoken to me but was topped off with a disapproving frown. At the time I didn't realize how negative of an impact that one moment would weigh in on my life and how I viewed myself.

Healing would not truly take place for many years to come.

I would have to go thru some trying times, do a total mental re-haul, dig deep into the word of God and totally surrender myself to God in a season of *total isolation.* It would just be me and Him. I would me listen to Him, cry out and simply ask Him to help me and *guide* me out of the wilderness of insecurities and bad decisions.

It was during this season of wilderness, that I discovered just how beautiful and strong, I really was.

My innate ability to pick myself up after I had fallen so hard on my face had transformed me into the woman that I have become today. Just having the sheer strength to resist the enemy while pulling myself out of my brokenness has been an incredible feat to me! My inner strength is what truly makes me beautiful not any external beauty.

That is how I want to be known.

The Music Industry

In my field of work ˜the Music industry, unfortunately your looks do play a major part in the success of your music. It can be very difficult for a recording artist to make a living by simply operating in their gift and putting out good content.

The Music industry has made it clear˜ the more attractive you are equals higher engagement and a bigger fanbase; which ultimately leads to more sales, streams and notoriety than an artist who is considered less attractive. Sadly, artists feel as if they are drowning in an oversaturated industry; where your ability to be heard is based on your following, your likes, and looks as the status quo.

Nevertheless, I have come to realize that God will give you favor when you operate solely in your gift to Glory Him alone and edify His people! So I rejoice in knowing that If God called me to it, then **I know without a shadow of a doubt** that He will guide me and give me provisions to succeed in this massive industry as I continuously strive to minister to His people.

Beauty Tip

Have you ever had a favorite eyebrow color that you thought would look good in a lipstick?

Well, all you have to do is mix the loose pigments from your eyebrow color with a little bit of *Vaseline (Petroleum Jelly)* in a spoon and then *swipe* it on your lips!

Boom!

The perfect lip color is served... It works every time.

Beauty Secret revealed

My beauty regimen is pretty simple.

In the mornings I wash my face with lukewarm water along with *Simple Foaming Facial Cleanser* to remove makeup/ dead skin cells and oils.

To keep my skin nice and clear (pimple free), I've adopted a stress-free lifestyle that includes the habit of drinking plenty of water. This habit ensures that my skin glows naturally without the aid of foundation.

#MustHaves

Eyebrows- *Anastia Beverly Hills* Brow Pencil in medium brown to fill in my brows

Eyes- *Morphe Gel Eyeliner* in midnight black to line my eyes.

Lipstick- *Mac Ruby Woo* for that bold pop of color!

#howiSlay

So how do I slay in my business?

Prayer, Coffee, Eyeliner and a lot of **Hustle**! I wouldn't get far without any of these -inserts laugh-

The more I *pray* and communicate with God, the more I feel myself transforming further into the God-Fearing woman He has always created me to be! Once I started to believe in myself, I became that fearless Woman in everything she does. Especially when it comes down to *slaying* my dreams and goals like the Queen that I am!

I've become more strategic in my decisions and always keep God involved in everything that I do. I always remind myself of not only who I am, but also who I belong to which is God and that never fails!

I'm following God's purpose for my life ON purpose and because of Him, I find myself *moving* and *flourishing* like never before!

Collect

I am very mindful to always start my day off with prayer.

It must be the very first thing that I do before my feet even touch the ground. Prayer for is a necessity for me to move and conquer the day. It gives me a great sense of peace to talk to God about my plans, dreams, and just to simply thank Him for another chance to do His will. I do not take my opportunity of life for granted. Every day He allows me to open my eyes is a blessing.

I always try to focus on the things that I can control while also maintaining a positive attitude. I've come a long way from the days of old where I always found myself stressing and entertaining negative thoughts towards circumstances and unexpected problems that I had no control over.

I now have extreme joy in knowing that real happiness and peace is only found in Christ Jesus. And because I've learned to truly trust Him in all things, I am truly able to live a joyful life.

My Hope for YOU

After reading this excerpt, my earnest prayer is that my story is the **key to unlocking another woman's prison**. May you be motivated to make each day your *masterpiece* as you follow Gods plan for your life. Know that you are beautiful in every way, and that you are wonderfully made. It is my prayer that you will evolve into a woman that is unafraid to be *herself*.

There is nothing more beautiful than that.

Sis, you need to know

Never let anyone make you believe that God can't use you because of your past mistakes. The same grace that was extended to them is the same grace that saved your life. You no longer need to convince anybody of God's plan for your life.

Just continue to MOVE forward with the peace in your soul that God has given you.

About the Author

Mika Morrow is an American Inspirational/ gospel singer and song-writer and Best-Selling Author. Born again and a bible believer, she is on a mission to impact lost souls who needs guidance and healing in today's world through the ministry of song. She has recently de-buted 2 new singles "Move" and "Showtime" which can be found on all digital outlets. She resides in Baltimore, Maryland with her adoring husband and 2 beautiful children.

Stay Connected with this Pray, Slay, & Collect Queen

Follow on FB @Tamika Morrow

IG @mikamorrow

Booking: bookmikamorrow@gmail.com

You Are SAVED

Queen,

You have officially been inspired to *Pray* about everything, *Slay* in All that you do, and positioned to *Collect* your peace, your joy, and All that God has instore for YOU! You understand the true meaning of beauty and just how bright and beautiful our Father created You to BE!

You are Challenged to Do Great and to Be GREAT in the body of Christ because you are fearfully and wonderfully made.

Now Sis, if you read these pages but still feel inadequate, unattractive and not yet worthy of love, I'd like to invite you to get to know a man by the name of Jesus!

He is better than your most trusted friend and will show you the True meaning of love and exquisite beauty!

Say this simple prayer to accept Christ into your life, and I believe, Our Lord and Savior will wrap His loving arms around you, embrace you, and show you Exactly what you've been searching for All along.

READ THIS ALOUD AND BELIEVE IN YOUR HEART

Heavenly Father,

I come to you now as humble as I know how.

I recognize that I am broken- in more ways than one. I need you Lord and I receive you on this day!

I am a sinner, in need of a Savoir.

I know that Jesus, you are that Savior.

You are the Son of God.

I know that you died for my sins and rose again on the 3rd day to give me life.

I ask for your forgiveness, your love, and embrace now.

I repent from my sins and will follow you for the rest of my life.

Make me new on this day Lord.

I believe it and receive it and I know that it is done.

In Jesus Name I say these things.

Amen!

Queen, I believe that if you said that prayer aloud and believe it in your heart- then you my Queen are SAVED! The Angels in Heaven are REJOICING for YOU and so are All my Boss Queens!

I encourage you Queen to find a great bible-based church or community that speaks and teaches the word of God from the Holy Bible. Find a community or a group of believers who will help guide you and steer you the right way. Continue to pray daily for God to make His plan for your life PLAIN. Ask Him to help you when you are weak and when you want to fall back into the destructive behaviors of your former self.

If you need help, need a prayer, or an encouraging word- Please feel free to email us over at jesuscoffeeandprayer@gmail.com

If you gave your life to Christ for the first time, or came back to Him on this day, we want to hear about it and CELEBRATE WITH YOU!

EMAIL US: jesuscoffeeandprayer@gmail.com

In the subject line type: SAVED

If you declare with your mouth, "Jesus is Lord," and believe in your heart that God raised him from the dead, you will be saved. Romans 10:9 NIV

Pray, Slay, COLLECT.

Moment of Reflection

How will You help another Queen Collect her Peace Today?

Final Prayer for You!

—

Lord, I Thank You- We Thank You for another opportunity to inspire, encourage, and edify your Daughters. We Thank You for the ability to use our stories, our prayers, our God-given wisdom to pour into your children. May every word written or said be received by the people You ordained to hear it- on this day!

We Speak Life

We Speak Favor

We Speak Resources and Overflow for your Daughters, their children and families too!

Bless them richly for picking up this book and being obedient to YOU- Your Word Can NEVER come back Void!

May our words, thoughts, and deeds be acceptable in your sight, as we are Good soil and You have planted Good seeds within us!

Bless your children some 10, some 30, some 60-fold.

In the Precious Name of Jesus, We Speak All of these things and More!

We love you Lord

Amen, Amen, & Amen again

Min. Nakita

You Shine Bright

—

You shine bright
I see how you glow
Your value is worth more than any Silver and Gold
-

You take care of hubby and you support your kids
Late nights- early mornings
Queen
You handle your biz
-

Messy hair
Don't care or
Slacks with business suit
-

You are a Queen on a Mission
You are winning in full pursuit
-

You've got vision
You've got sass
-

You're the kinda Queen popping with all that jazz
-

Your haters stay mad but you could care less
You are about your Fathers business
Ain't got time for no stress!
-

Blessed and highly favored is your nick name
This is chess -not checkers &

You're the Queen of this Game

-

-

Your heels are high
But your Faith remains higher

-

You acknowledge our God
Our one and only Sire

-

While people complain
Queen -you cash checks

-

No need to worry
Your accountant handles that!

-

Your primer is on point & your lashes stay long
& with God on your side
Queen you are never alone

-

-

If nobody tells you
Sis I'm proud of you
You take care of your family
Because that's what real bosses do!

-

You're loyal to God
And You serve your community
Your Faith is on 10

Just like a REAL Queen should be!

I love you Sis
Min. Nakita

READY TO TAKE THE LEAP OF FAITH AND BECOME A BEST-SELLING QUEEN CO-AUTHOR TOO!

TEXT: PUBLISHME TO 31996

&

Schedule a FREE 20min. Book Consultation TODAY

Just Mention Promo Code* PRAYSLAYCOLLECT *